# origins

Well-dressing almost certainly originated in pagan sacrifices to water-gods as a thanksgiving for past supplies and an inducement for further favours. Finding the sacrifice of humans and animals wasteful and sometimes distressing, primitive man adopted the more economical, colourful practice of hanging garlands of flowers above springs, as some South American Indian tribes still hang torn strips of coloured cotton for the same purpose.

*Elmton's dressing of 'Little Bo-Peep'*

The Romans made similar offerings to the gods at the Saturnalia and other pagan festivals, and there is a theory that they brought th[is] ... Derbyshire. Against that it must be said that nothing quite like our well-dressing survives in modern Italy. The nearest to it is perhaps at Genzano, south of Rome, where, writes Dr. Laura Oliveti of the Institute of Italian Culture, 'the flowers are arranged in a vast pattern on the street running through the centre of the town, not on a board, as in Derbyshire'.

More probably the custom is of pre-Roman, Celtic origin. Some anthropologists believe that Celtic strains survived successive invasions of Romans, Saxons, Danes and Normans in the remote hills of the Peak, and that even today the true Peaklander is of Celtic descent. His culture may also have lingered on longer than elsewhere.

# Religious Links

The early Christian Church handled pagan customs sensitively, absorbing and adapting rather than suppressing. That this was a slow process is clear from a decree of 960 expressly forbidding the worship of fountains. As late as 1102, St. Anselm was still condemning 'this form of idolatory'.

But well-dressing today has strong religious links. Probably three out of every four pictures have a religious theme. A service, usually inter-denominational, of blessing the wells is held everywhere. Often the clergy go in procession to each well in turn. There are well-dressers who see their work as closely akin to a harvest festival offering.

all things bright & beautiful

19 FOOLOW 95

# Why Dress Wells?

## Joy in CREATION

oney-raising is rarely the main motive for dressing wells, though considerable sums are given to both national and local charities from the collecting boxes perched unobtrusively near most wells. Why, then, do people willingly give up a week each year to the dressing?

Some, like the Shimwells of Youlgrave and the Needhams of Barlow, among other families, are born into it. Others find it gives them a new sense of achievement. 'For people with the creative urge but no great ability, it offers a chance to achieve aesthetic satisfaction,' in the words of Jim Shimwell, Secretary of the Youlgrave Well-Dressing Association. For newcomers it offers an entry into village life. Most dressers enjoy the comradeship and the carnival atmosphere and many are anxious to preserve an ancient custom which is also a genuine folk-art.

But most, I suspect, cannot define why they do it. As with painting, or writing, or climbing Everest, or sailing single-handed round the world, it is simply a challenge that they cannot resist.

*Above:*
*The centrepiece of a*
*dressing at Dronfield*
*Woodhouse*

*Gray's Elegy at*
*the village of*
*Brackenfield*

# Why Derbyshire?

why has well-dressing survived almost exclusively in Derbyshire? The answer would have been easier to deduce 50 years ago when only about 14 places dressed their wells than it is today with three times that number observing the custom.

A glance at a geological map would have shown that nearly all those villages stood on mountain limestone, which is slightly porous. Within half an hour of a heavy storm the soil will be dry, the water having seeped through to the subterranean natural cistern that underlies the limestone.

In such an area, springs were vital. Early hill settlements were invariably sited where one or more springs emerged. If the spring failed, so did the village economy. Life itself was in jeopardy.

That explains two rival theories for the beginning, or revival, of well-dressing at Tissington. One is that the purity of the spring-water preserved the villagers of Tissington during the Black Death of 1348-49, in which 77 of the 100 beneficed clergy in Derbyshire are known to have died. The second is that the Tissington wells kept flowing in a prolonged drought in the summer of 1615 when 'the greatest part of the land was burnt up, both corn and hay'. One can see why the villagers may have performed a half-forgotten act of thanksgiving in either circumstance. Both indeed may be true, the drought possibly serving as a reminder of a custom that had lapsed.

What is certain is that in 1758, Nicholas Hardinge, Clerk of the House of Commons, saw at Tissington 'springs adorned with garlands . . . in honour of these fountains, which . . . are annually commemorated on Holy Thursday'.

In 1794 the Gentleman's Magazine observed that 'In the village of Tissington . . . it has been a custom, time immemorial, on every Holy Thursday, to decorate the wells with boughs of trees, garlands of tulips and other flowers, placed in various fancied devices; and after prayers for the day at the church, for the parson and singers to pray and sing psalms at the wells', which is not very different from what still happens. But if that 'time immemorial' means no more than the memory of the oldest inhabitant's grandparents, it would still carry us back into the second half of the 17th century, which is probably when some form of well-dressing would have started up again, after being banned, as it surely would have been, by the Puritans.

*On this page are various details from the dressings at Baslow, Brackenfield, Elmton, Foolow, Hartington and Monyash*

# How is it Done?

*No two places assemble their wells in quite the same way, so*

*Boards soak in the village pond; we follow the progress of the Tissington Dressers*

*The heavy screens are hauled away to begin the work*

*The clay is 'puddled' with water and salt to a uniform consistency*

The first requirement is a strong boarded framework of five or six units, usually made locally. They can be expected to require some attention, or even renewal, every five years or so, but some last much longer. These heavy screens - 'about as big as a barn door' at Tissington - are dressed separately and hauled to the wells behind a tractor.

Long before that, however, the screens will have been soaked - in the village pond at Tissington - and covered with clay, dug locally if possible. This clay is puddled with water and salt to a uniform plastic consistency, and then applied as a layer from half to an inch thick to all units of the framework. The salt will keep the clay moist to prevent cracking in wind and sun as well as preserving the freshness of flowers. Hundreds of nails protruding about a quarter of an inch from the board help to 'key' the clay.

The drawing, previously prepared full-size on paper, is then applied to the smooth surface of the clay, and the design pricked through

# Bakewell

## *Five wells dressed on the last Saturday in June*

This charming market town, the only one in the Peak District National Park, makes a good centre for a well-dressing tour. Tradition says well-dressing flourished in the early 18th century when the town had aspirations to become a spa, but its revival dates only from 1971 when the British Legion (Women's Section), with advice and help from Ashford-in-the-Water, dressed the warm well (a constant 58°F) at their headquarters, Bath House.

Much progress has been made since those days. Men now participate; a postmaster and a retired police sergeant soon developed into particularly skilled craftsmen, as did some enthusiastic young people. All five wells are dressed in the same room harmoniously and to such good effect that two dressings were displayed before the Queen Mother at the Chelsea Flower Show in 1977.

# Barlow

## Three wells dressed on the Wednesday after the Sunday after St. Lawrence's Day (August 10)

Barlow has probably dressed its main well for longer than any other well outside the limestone area. As at Tissington, the well provided water through the 1615 drought, and one theory is that the dressings began as a thanks-offering. Others think the custom may be as old as the annual Feast celebrating St. Lawrence's Day (the patronal festival of the village church) that has been observed since at least Elizabeth I's reign, as the earliest church register of 1572 testifies. This well has certainly been dressed - without a break even in two wars - throughout living memory. Wilfred Needham has worked at it for 'over 60 years and we'll leave it at that', following in his father's footsteps as a grandson and a great-grandson are now following his. Several other village families have similarly lengthy well-dressing traditions.

Dressing is always done at the well behind a tarpaulin canopy over scaffold poles hiding the open front of the stone well-house erected in 1840 and given to the village by the Duke of Rutland in 1927. Weight is the reason. Three screens - each 4½ ft. long - are used with a different picture on each.

### Barlow

Four screens used to be employed and still are from time to time. On one memorable occasion a single picture of the Last Supper was spread over all four. Even singly, the Barlow pictures are above average weight because the clay is thicker to take whole flowers instead of petals. 'We don't believe flowers were created to be torn up,' one dresser put it. The rule about using 'only growing things' is very strictly observed. Rambler roses, asters, stocks and wild yarrow are extensively used.

*The main well is erected around the old village pump which dates back to 1840*

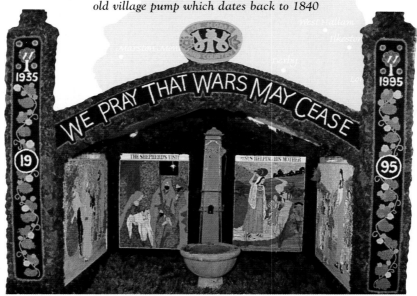

# Bonsall

*Three wells at least, and children's wells, dressed for carnival week, usually the last Saturday in July.*

Bonsall

*Above and below: Religious scenes at Bonsall*

The number of wells dressed varies slightly in this long hill-village, but the standard of dressing is always high. Only natural materials are used - 'no bits of gravel' - but hair, both human and sheep, is accepted, as is desiccated coconut. But most of what is likely to be needed - hydrangeas, marigolds, golden tiger-lilies, delphiniums - are grown in village gardens or found around local lanes. Among the latter are the seeds of immature elderberries (soaked first, or the wet clay makes them swell and pop out), docks, aniseed (oven dried to a golden brown), or alder cones which are gathered a year in advance.

The designers try to avoid formal designs. The most recent screen, made by a former Rector, is in triptych form, as at Barlow. Another resemblance to Barlow is the use of whole feverfew flowers, which are plentiful locally, in place of the usual petals.

# Bradwell

*Four wells are dressed to coincide with Carnival Day on the Saturday before the first Monday in August (the Old Bank Holiday).*

There are vague memories of well-dressing 'back at the beginning of the century' in this former lead-mining village, but the present series began in 1949 when the Bowling Green Well was dressed for Smalldale Wakes. The Wakes are no longer held and the wells are now dressed for Carnival Day and remain on view throughout the Gala Week that follows, when there are exhibitions in the Parish Church and the Methodist Church.

The method of dressing is unusual. Instead of pricking the outlines of the picture into the clay, the dressers lay the picture on the clay and cut out a section line by line with razor blades. They petal that section before exposing more clay, thus keeping it moist. The outlines are completed with dried seeds of sweet cicely.

*'Protect and Survive'*
*Marine Conservation*

'No garden is sacred' in the search for flowers, but only natural materials are used, including lots of dead leaves and lichens.

Villagers and visitors parade behind a band on the Sunday evening after Carnival Day for the Blessing of each well by the Vicar and the Methodist Minister. All money collected at the wells is given to Bradwell senior citizens in the form of vouchers at Christmas.

*A ten year commemoration of 'Live Aid' with the story of Lazarus – the man who rose from the dead*

*The story of Noah's Ark tops the school's dressing of 1995*

# Etwall

## Eight wells dressed in mid-May

This most southerly of Derbyshire's well-dressing villages adopted the custom almost by chance. Teachers marked the centenary of the village primary school in 1970 by dressing a token 'well', while the Women's Institute, with help and advice from Tissington and Youlgrave, dressed Etwall's only true well, Town Well, probably the *Eata's* well from which the village derived its name.

These 'one off' ventures proved so successful that a Well-Dressing Association was formed to administer what has since been an annual event which attracts crowds of visitors.

*Using a variety of motifs: Prince of Wales' feathers and biblical sphinxes, Etwall's Egginton Well commemorates 50 years of peace*

*Schools take a very active part in well-dressing*

Another reason may be that the very absence of a well-dressing tradition has enabled dressers to tackle entirely fresh subjects. Racial unity, symbolised by crossed black and white arms, was one theme; another was the life and times of Sir John Port, once of Etwall Hall, founder of Repton School and of the almshouses near the church.

## Etwall

Each well is the responsibility of a separate organisation, but the social effect of well-dressing has been to unify a village at a time of exceptionally rapid growth.

One reason for this success is that Etwall's geographical position on the lowlands south of the Peak ensures an earlier growth of flowers than is usual farther north, thus enabling it to take an early place in the well-dressing calendar.

*The Women's Institute celebrates 250 years of Bonnie Prince Charlie*

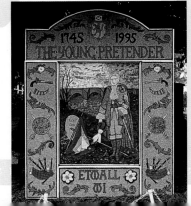

# Eyam

## Three wells dressed last Saturday in August.

Well-dressing has especial poignancy here, for it commemorates the heroism of its people in the 1665-66 plague which killed 257 of them; about a third of the population. Inspired by the rector, William Mompesson, and his ejected nonconforming predecessor, Thomas Stanley, they prevented the disease spreading by staying in the parish. Incoming supplies were delivered to places on the outskirts, like Mompesson's Well, where coins in payment were placed in water, with vinegar added as a disinfectant.

Church services were held in the open in Cucklet Delf, as they still are on the last Sunday in August – Plague Sunday – which commemorates the plague's climax and the death of the rector's wife, Catherine Mompesson.

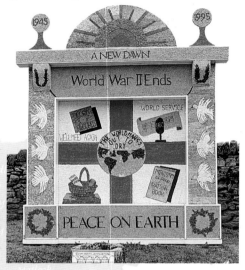

That well-dressing is tied to this late date restricts the choice of flowers, but Eyam dressers invariably overcome the problems of Peakland's early autumns.

Town Head Well is thought to have the biggest screens in the Peak. Its picture board is nine feet wide and nearly six feet tall. It tends to display a topical picture, whereas the other two wells more often have Biblical scenes, though scenes commemorating the Eyam Plague of 1665-6 are not infrequent, as one might well expect.

Local writer and historian Clarence Daniel wrote a well-dressing hymn to be sung at the service, with another for children.

*Above:*
*Another version of the peace theme*

*Left:*
*A highly decorative design surrounded by the fruits of the earth*

# Heath, Ault Hucknall, Glapwell & Rowthorne

*Four wells (one at each village) dressed on the third Saturday in July.*

When Rowthorne took up well-dressing for the first time in 1995, Heath, on the east side of the Doe Lea Valley and the M1, reverted to running its own well-dressing affairs instead of combining, as it had done for some years, with the villages on the west side which are all in the ecclesiastical parish of Ault Hucknall. The split was entirely amicable and for ease of administration; the wells, roughly two miles apart, continue to be displayed at the same time.

There was no previous tradition of well-dressing in these east Derbyshire villages when in 1975 Mr. Tom Price, then in charge of adult education locally, found inspiration at Bonsall, advice at Marsh Lane and Ashford and the co-operation in his villages which encouraged him to launch what he saw as a folk-art form within the scope of most adult students.

*Above: admiring Heath's Dressing*

*Right: another biblical story at Ault Hucknall*

None of the 40 wells in the area is suitably located for dressing so false ones are dressed on boards twice the usual size and rectangular, because the village carpenter who made them mislaid the dimensions supplied by Marsh Lane. Most of the dressers are women and children. Every child in Heath also helps to dress an additional children's well in the Vicarage garden. Lisa Stimpson, who has designed the Heath dressings since 1985, teaches art. She always chooses to illustrate a familiar religious text, as do the dressers at Ault Hucknall where the board is immediately outside the south porch of the lovely early-Norman church in which the philosopher Thomas Hobbes is buried.

*'Moses in the Bullrushes' – a dressing at Rowthorne*

# Holymoorside

## Two wells dressed on the Wednesday before the late Summer Bank Holiday.

The dressers at Holymoorside are amongst the many whose initial training came from the ever-helpful Barlow craftsmen and continue to use the same methods. That was in 1979, when the custom was revived in the village after a gap of around 80 years, the exact year it ceased having been forgotten. It was certainly being observed in 1890 when the Lamb Inn was advertising that 'Its Annual Well-Dressings' would take place on Feast Tuesday and Wednesday, July 1st and 2nd. 'A large marquee' was to be erected in a nearby field, and it was presumably in that that the Cutthorpe Brass Band was playing for Dancing each evening from 7pm. Earlier in the 19th century, it is believed that the Whistling Well and Penny Well, along with perhaps one other, had been dressed.

Nowadays two wells are dressed on the same site: a large one – nearly 12ft by 9ft – for the adults and another of less than half that size for the children. Dressing starts on the Monday before August Bank Holiday and visitors who accept a general invitation to watch the dressers at work on the site will notice that the Barlow tradition of using flowers and leaves only is strictly observed; wool, seeds, shells and the like are out. The work is normally completed on the Wednesday and remains on view for the next 10 days to coincide with the Village Gala on the Saturday before Bank Holiday and the 4-day church craft exhibition over the holiday weekend. The dressers believe that their most spectacular effort so far was their 1990 picture commemorating the 50th anniversary of the Battle of Britain. Photographs of it in national newspapers rewarded 400 hours of effort.

*Hopscotch being played outside the village school*

Children had always been encouraged to help on the other wells. In fact all hands are required if a village of fewer than 200 people, many of them in far-flung farms, is to dress five wells. That is one of Tissington's main problems, but one they invariably overcome. The villagers divide themselves into five teams by a sort of natural selection. Nobody bothers much what the other teams are doing, though there is no attempt at secrecy now as there once was. There may nowadays even be a certain amount of interchanging of materials, but there is no attempt to avoid a possible clashing of themes. In fact, only twice in living memory have two wells clashed and then their treatment was so different that it hardly mattered.

A more worrying problem is a possible shortage of flowers so early in the season 800 ft. up on the limestone in a region where winters can be long and hard. It means that dressers have to go farther afield than most villages to collect their materials. Bluebells, if the season is not too early, are valuable, so are wallflowers, wild hyacinths and, with luck, rhododendrons, but daffodil and polyanthus petals soon fade in the clay. Alder cones, gathered in advance, are used for outlines. Fluorspar is used, but the spraying of white spar is considered 'unsporting', as is the use of dyed, artificial flowers which has been tried in the distant past. More use now is made of cultivated flowers, especially hydrangeas for skies, and red geraniums, both bought from Osmaston but becoming now disturbingly expensive. Coffee beans are used for fine work. Despite the limitations imposed by nature and a desire to stick fairly strictly to the rule about 'only natural materials', Tissington does well. Its pictures may be less colourful than in villages whose wells are dressed in mid-summer; human features may be less sharp than in places where strict rules are waived, but the Tissington dressers are generally admired by the experts and by their thousands of visitors.

*A biblical story, The Red Cross and the end of World War II combine to make an unusual display at the Hands Well*

# Wirksworth

## Approximately nine wells dressed from the Saturday before the late Spring Bank Holiday

Tap Dressings they were called when Wirksworth first adopted the custom in 1827 to celebrate the installation of a water supply. Although the original seven street taps have long gone and the boards do not in every case commemorate their sites, the dressings flourish under the more traditional name.

Well-dressing is indeed immensely popular at Wirksworth, as has always been the intention of its promoters. They have changed its date several times in order to draw the greatest number of visitors, who, with nine wells and a Well-Dressing Queen to admire and a carnival spirit abroad, are amply rewarded.

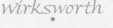

*Two dressings on 'Green' themes of conservation and natural history*

Reward also used to be sought by the dressers, for there was a strongly competitive element. Years ago, Susan Marsden, of Warmbrook, left £100, the interest to be divided annually as the prizes for wells dressed solely by the children. This led to funds being raised for adult prizes also, and to a rather unhealthy form of competition.

Consequently, the adult prizes were dropped, but for a time a panel still selected the four best boards on view and the overall winner was presented with a silver cup, but even that whiff of competition was abandoned a few years ago. However, it is worth mentioning that what the judges looked for then were:

1.   Subject and interpretation,
2.   Design, colour and originality,
3.   Craftsmanship,
4.   Overall impression.

25 marks were available under each heading.

Over the years the 'senior citizens' were the most successful dressers, but the most skilful of all was Isaac Gratton, who in the days of individual awards took first prize in 36 of his 38 attempts.

The judges kept strictly to the 'only what grows naturally' principle. A team of dressers who gave glass eyes to the main figures were not considered for a prize.

*A design symbolising the four gospels*

*A Triptych portraying the healing of the man at the pool of Siloam.*
*'Take up thy bed and walk'.*
*(John V. Verses 1–15)*

# Wormhill

## One well dressed from the Saturday before the late Summer Bank Holiday

A single well may not sound sufficient inducement for the trouble of reaching this small, remote village – no more than a string of stone-built farmhouses along a minor road 1,000 ft. up, above the former Millers Dale station. But thousands of people make an annual pilgrimage to Wormhill, leaving behind them up to £2,000 to be given jointly to the church and to the village hall fund, which could be a county record for one well.

There are several reasons for this popularity. One is the attractiveness of the village and its superb surroundings, though the largest limestone quarry in Europe is only just out of sight over the next hill. Another is the historic interest of the well itself, its stonework erected in 1895 as a slightly belated memorial to the great canal engineer James Brindley (1716-72), who was born in the parish at Tunstead. A third reason is that Mr. Oliver Shimwell, whose wife was a Wormhill native, designed and drew the picture. When he accepted the original invitation in 1951 to inaugurate its well-dressing he took over his Tideswell board and some of his team and he continued to supervise the Wormhill dressers until 1994. He is still a member of the well-dressing committee.

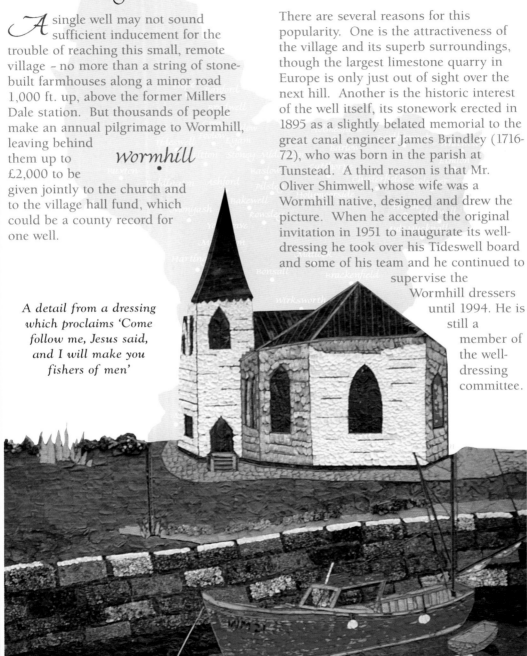

*A detail from a dressing which proclaims 'Come follow me, Jesus said, and I will make you fishers of men'*

# Youlgrave

## Five wells dressed from the Saturday nearest to St. John the Baptist Day (June 24)

More than most places, Youlgrave has reason for thanksgiving, being one of a few English villages with its own water undertaking. It was to celebrate the arrival of the first soft-water supply in iron pipes from a spring outside the village to the newly erected stone-enclosed reservoir known locally as The Fountain, that the first dressing probably took place in 1829.

The Reading Room Well

*A colourful version of the story of Joseph and Potiphar at Holywell*

The Fountain, tradition says, continued to be dressed for about 20 years before interest lapsed, to be revived in 1869 when a second waterworks scheme introduced several taps along the village street. These were decorated, while The Fountain received more elaborate treatment.

The present five 'wells' - the term is loosely used - were dressed in 1894 under the stimulus of prizes for the best dressings. When these were dropped, the dressers went professional, dividing amongst themselves the profits from the collecting boxes, usually about £2 a dresser.

Nowadays, the collections go to charity, but the standard of work is professional. Much of the credit for this exceptionally

high standard of dressing must go to the imaginative skills, allied to professional art training, which Mrs. Margaret Fell brought with her when she returned to her native village in the 1950s. Although the purists may object that she bends the rules, the visitor probably feels that the ends justify the means. Certainly the Youlgrave dressers are in great demand for advice and help from other well-dressers, not all of them local. Youlgrave dressers have twice given well-dressing displays at Darmstadt in Germany, and in 1982 Jim Shimwell and his wife gave demonstrations at Hatfield House, the Hertfordshire seat of the Marquess of Salisbury.

*Bank Top Well*

# other wells

BAMFORD still follows methods employed at neighbouring Hope which they learned from Dave Sanders who helped them in their initial well-dressing in 1991. Villagers of all ages are encouraged to participate in dressing the single well for the village carnival in mid-July.

St James's Day (July 25) is the patronal festival of BARLBOROUGH Church. The well is blessed that evening, if it happens to be Friday, or on the Friday following, and it stays dressed until the next Tuesday or Wednesday, coinciding with the church flower festival. Before the Young Wives Group started modestly with a small picture in 1975 there was no well-dressing tradition in this village close by the M 1's Junction 30. About 20 members of this organisation now do a more polished job with a design conceived by Tom Finney, a professional graphic designer.

A Brackenfield well-dressing

With a similar lack of tradition and experienced guidance, BASLOW'S first dressing - inspired by a talk from Joe Smith of Hope - was undertaken in 1984 entirely by beginners to raise funds for a local sports organisation. Now, under keen scrutiny from an established Well-Dressing Committee, a high standard has been reached at the main well on Goose Green and the work on the children's well outside the thatched cottages by the river suggests that the standard will be maintained. Both wells are on view around the first week in July.

BRACKENFIELD'S original wells on Derbyshire's largest village green are now covered over and their substitutes are scattered around the village, attracting attention when they are dressed from Spring Bank Holiday Saturday until the following Tuesday. The earliest designs in 1986 were strongly influenced by the work done at Tissington, but the local volunteers, helped by the Clay Cross Arts Group, are sufficiently confident now to do their own thing, usually on a pre-selected scheme. Two local schools, Wessington and Ashover, do a well each, leaving the other to the adults.

Although tap dressing took place in CHESTERFIELD in the 19th century, its 20th century revival as well-dressing began as late as 1991 when a well was dressed for a local traditions exhibition in the Peacock Heritage Centre.

Members of the Holymoorside well-dressing group helped with this first dressing, passing on techniques they had themselves inherited from their Barlow mentors, such as using whole flower-heads, though that method was dropped after two years and petals are now used. The Chesterfield dressers are now establishing their own traditions. Those at the Peacock Centre use buildings for their theme, while their colleagues at the 'Crooked Spire' church (St Mary and All Saints) have been basing their work on designs from stained glass windows in the church. At these two venues, where the dressing is done on site, visitors are welcome to watch work in progress in early September; the other two sites are less accessible.

The hillside village of *CRESSBROOK* now dresses a well on the Green for its Gala Week about the first week in June.

Although now within the city of Sheffield, the former Derbyshire village of *DORE* has continued to dress a well on its village green in the second week of July since 1959.

*ELMTON* well-dressing has been held annually at the weekend nearest to St Peter's Day (June 29), the Patronal Festival of the parish church, since 1986. An important but incidental result of the event is that it has bound together the two strands of the combined parish of Elmton and Creswell.

*FOOLOW* began well-dressing in 1983 to raise funds for a new village hall. Two boards are dressed - one by children - at the single well on the Green. Unusually, the design is drawn straight onto the clay. The dressings are displayed from the last Saturday in August, coinciding with Wakes Week and nearby Eyam's well-dressing.

Like Tissington, *GREAT HUCKLOW* avoids the usual Saturday opening of its

well-dressing. The well in what, despite its name, is one of the smallest of well-dressing villages, is dressed for the second Monday in August, two days before Gala Day.

Although lying on limestone in the lovely Dove Valley, *HARTINGTON* dressed no well before about 1980. Annually ever since, on Wakes Saturday, the second Saturday in September, dressed screens have been erected on a green overlooking the village mere, thus ending the well-dressing season that traditionally opens at nearby Tissington on Ascension Day.

*HEAGE* has dressed no well since 1989, but there are hopes of an early revival.

Two separate well-dressings take place at different dates in the large, scattered parish of *HOLMESFIELD*. One opens about the last Saturday in July in the hamlet of *MILLTHORPE,* where a team of ladies with a male designer, revived in 1979 a custom which had lapsed before 1939. Initially helped by Barlow dressers, they naturally follow the techniques employed there. *COWLEY* starts its well-dressing about the third or fourth Thursday in June to coincide with the Flower Festival in the Mission Church, which is one of about 16 churches around Dronfield that have their Flower Festivals over the same week-end.

The 50th anniversary of the opening of *MARSTON MONTGOMERY'S* village hall led to the revival of well-dressing there after a lapse of 49 years. When it was decided in 1987 to dress the village well - now a bus stop near the church - the event was intended as a 'one off' celebration of the hall's half century and not the revival of a custom last practised in 1938. But the dressing proved so enjoyable and to have such a unifying effect in a village then in transition that it is now an annual event about the second week-end in June. Proceeds are divided equally between the maintenance of the hall and a charity selected annually. A selection of photographs of each year's events is on display in the village's only inn *The Crown*.

The current revival of well-dressing at *MIDDLETON-BY-YOULGRAVE* began in 1977 to celebrate the Queen's Jubilee, after a gap of 80 years since Queen Victoria's Diamond Jubilee in 1897. The well is now dressed for the Spring Bank Holiday Saturday, the day of Middleton's major fund-raising event – the Village Market.

*MONYASH* first dressed Newton Well with boards, clay and general help from Litton in 1974. The dressing now has more space on the adjacent car park, a product of the successful integrated Rural Development Project. A children's well near the school is now also dressed. Both wells are on view from the Saturday before Monyash holds its own village Market on the Green on Spring Bank Holiday Monday, two days after Middleton.

Well-dressing came to *PEAK FOREST* in 1994 when the villagers decided to hold a Festival about the third week in July as a major community fund-raising effort. Well-dressing was to be a major attraction, despite the absence of any inhabitant with practical experience of the craft. But they found a retired art teacher with ideas, a few tips in surrounding villages, and in Tideswell they found clay that had been used for its

*The School's dressing at Peak Forest*

own boards, which Peak Forest borrowed to see it through its first dressing. Two wells are dressed, one by the children with adult supervision and a parent who is also an art student as designer. The wells - taps, literally - are blessed on the evening of the first day of the dressings (a Wednesday) after a procession.

About mid-July, St Michael's Church, *PLEASLEY,* has a well-dressing coinciding with its Flower Festival.

*TADDINGTON* took up Well-dressing in 1990 to provide an additional attraction in the annual Flower Festival week (the week before the late Summer Bank Holiday), hoping to raise extra money for repairs to the ancient parish church. Lacking first-hand knowledge of the craft, some potential key dressers gained experience by helping to dress Ashford's wells. Taddington dresses two wells. The aptly named High Well is dressed entirely by the village children. Standing 1200 ft upon the hillside above Taddington, and offering superb views, it supplied the village with water until the 1950s, the water flowing down a series of 'water